WORKBOOK

John Wiltshier • José Luis Morales
Series Advisor: David Nunan

Series Consultants:
Hilda Martínez • Xóchitl Arvizu

Advisory Board:
Tim Budden • Tina Chen • Betty Deng
Aaron Jolly • Dr. Nam-Joon Kang
Dr. Wonkey Lee • Wenxin Liang
Ann Mayeda • Wade O. Nichols
Jamie Zhang

T0346222

Pearson Education Limited
Edinburgh Gate
Harlow
Essex CM20 2JE
England
and Associated Companies throughout the world.

Our Discovery Island ™

www.ourdiscoveryisland.com

First published 2012
ISBN: 978-1-4479-0071-9

Eleventh impression 2020
Fourteenth impression 2022

Set in Longman English 16/21pt
Printed in Slovakia by Neografia

Based on the work of Fiona Beddall

Illustrators: Charlotte Alder (The Bright Agency), Fred Blunt, Lawrence Christmas, Leo Cultura, Mark Draisey, John Martz, Simone Massoni (Advocate Art), Rob McClurkan (Beehive Illustration), Ken Mok, Olimpia Wong

Picture Credits: The publisher would like to thank the following for their kind permission to reproduce their photographs: (Key: b-bottom; c-centre; l-left; r-right; t-top) Alamy Images: Image Source 33, ImageState 76, Profimedia International s.r.o. 20 (bicycle), vario images GmbH & Co.KG 43l; Bridgeman Art Library Ltd: Alte Pinakothek, Munich, Germany 13; Trevor Clifford: 20 (Matt); Corbis: dpa / Sven Simon 81c, Patrik Giardino 73, Imaginechina 81b, Paul Souders 43r, Ultimate Chase / Mike Theiss 39; iStockphoto: Cristian Andrei Matei 20 (football); Photolibrary.com: Brand X Pictures 32; Rex Features: Image Source 20 (skateboard), WestEnd61 20 (Jamie); Shutterstock.com: Apollofoto 35bl, 85tr, Yuri Arcurs 6/2, 35br, 85tl, Artpose Adam Borkowski 55c, Andi Berger 35tl, Franck Boston 25/3, cabania 20 (Sasha), Christo 21b, Clearviewstock 79/2, Willee Cole 55r, David Davis 45 (Maria), 79/3, Jaimie Duplass 45 (Peter), East 45 (Sofia), Gelpi 25/1, Grafica 85br, Simon Greig 25tl, Dr. Le Thanh Hung 79/6, Jaggat 6/1, Naluwan 6/6, 45 (George), Palmer Kane LLC 45 (John), Thomas M Perkins 6/5, 35cl, Privilege 45 (Jenny), Red-Blue Photo 85bl, Brad Sauter 35tr, SergiyN 25/2, Sheftsoff 6/4, Ljupco Smokovski 45 (Sandra), Wong Sze Yuen 6/3, thefinalmiracle 79/1, Leah-Anne Thompson 45 (Diego), Tikona 79/5, Veronika Trofer 81t, Tomasz Trojanowski 55l, Tracy Whiteside 21t, 25/4, Arman Zhenikeyev 79/4

All other images © Pearson Education

Every effort has been made to trace the copyright holders and we apologise in advance for any unintentional omissions. We would be pleased to insert the appropriate acknowledgement in any subsequent edition of this publication.

Contents

Welcome

1 Write the names of the characters.

> Jenny   Rufus   Captain Formosa   Dylan   Ivan   Dr. Al   Finn

1

2

3

4

_____ _____ _____ _____

5

6

7

_____ _____ _____

2 Look at Activity 1 and number the sentences.

a He's wearing boots and a hat.
He likes skiing, snowboarding, and rock climbing. `6`

b He has a white mustache and a blue hat.
He likes penguins and he lives in an old submarine. ☐

c He's short and fat. He likes diving and he's strong. ☐

d He's tall and thin. He likes running and wants to find the treasure. ☐

e She likes adventure and has a backpack full of useful things.
She's wearing a skirt. ☐

f He has a beard and brown hair.
He likes watching the stars and planets. ☐

g He has glasses and is wearing a coat and a scarf.
He likes to think and solve problems. ☐

3  Check (✓).

1 What is Dr. Al studying?

a   b   c

☐   ☐   ☐

2 Who gets the map?

a   b   c

☐   ☐   ☐

4 Circle T = True or F = False.

1 Finn, Jenny, and Dylan wake up in the middle of the night.   T / F

2 Jenny sees a rabbit on the moon.   T / F

3 Captain Formosa is sleeping in the submarine.   T / F

4 The penguins are in the submarine, too.   T / F

5 The penguins see the thieves.   T / F

6 The thieves are hiding with the map.   T / F

5 (02) Listen and match. Then write.

1 What is Finn doing?   _____

2 What is Dylan doing?   _____

3 What is Jenny doing?   _____

6 🖊 **Write.**

a She is _____ .

b They _____ baseball.

c _____

d _____

e _____

f _____

g _____

h _____ the piano.

7 🔘03 **Listen and match**

8 🖊 **Look at Activity 7 and write.**

| watched   listened   practiced   played   went   studied |

1 She _____ to some music on Monday morning.

2 He _____ English on Thursday morning.

3 They _____ volleyball on Saturday afternoon.

4 She _____ a soccer game on Wednesday evening.

5 They _____ to the park on Sunday afternoon.

6 He _____ the guitar on Tuesday evening.

9 ✏️ **Write the days.**

1 Yesterday was _____. Today is Tuesday.

2 Today is Saturday. Tomorrow is _____.

3 Two days ago was _____. Today is Thursday.

10 ✏️ **Write the years.**

Now it's 20____ ____. Two years ago it was 20____ ____.

Ten years ago it was 20 ____ ____.

11 04 **Listen and match. Then write.**

① ② ③ ④ ⑤ LIBRARY

| on Monday morning | | two years ago | | three days ago |

| two weeks ago | | yesterday |

1 She _____ at school _____.

2 He _____.

3 They _____.

4 She _____ that _____.

5 They _____.

12 ✏️ **Write about yourself.**

1 I _____ yesterday.

2 I _____ on _____.

3 I _____ ago.

7

1 Friends

1 Unscramble and write.

Hair:

1 (hgilt raih) _____

2 (ladb) _____

3 (yksip iarh) _____

4 (kdra hria) _____

Face:

5 (etcu) _____

6 (mdnaheos) _____

7 (odgo-gkolnio) _____

8 (auultibef) _____

2 Write. Use words from Activity 1.

1
I have _____ hair.
Emma

2
I have _____ hair.
Maddy

3
I have _____ hair.
Robbie

4
I'm _____.
Dan

3 Write one more sentence for each picture in Activity 2.

1 _____

2 _____

3 _____

4 _____

4 **Unscramble and write questions.**

1 does / look / what / she / like _____

2 look / what / do / like / they _____

3 look / does / he / what / like _____

5 **Circle. Then check (✓) the true sentences.**

a

1 He (is / has) bald. ☐

2 He (is / has) long, straight hair. ☐

b

1 She (has / is) beautiful. ☐

2 She (has / is) glasses. ☐

c

1 They (are / have) tall. ☐

2 They (are / have) short, curly hair. ☐

6 **05** **Listen and write.**

	Dad	Mom	Grandpa
hair	bald		
eyes			
other			

7 **Write sentences about the people in Activity 6.**

1 Dad is bald. He has _____.

2 Mom _____.

3 Grandpa _____.

8 Match.

1 She has a lot of friends because

2 She has a lot of friends but

3 She has a lot of friends and

4 I'm tall because

5 I'm tall but

6 I'm tall and

a she doesn't have any brothers or sisters.

b she has a lot of pets.

c she's funny and kind.

d I have straight black hair.

e my mom and dad are tall.

f I'm not two meters tall!

9 Check (✓).

What makes a good friend?

	a good friend	don't mind	a bad friend
1 This person is friendly.	☐	☐	☐
2 This person isn't kind.	☐	☐	☐
3 This person is clever.	☐	☐	☐
4 This person isn't talkative.	☐	☐	☐
5 This person is bossy.	☐	☐	☐
6 This person is shy.	☐	☐	☐
7 This person isn't sporty.	☐	☐	☐
8 This person is lazy.	☐	☐	☐
9 This person is helpful.	☐	☐	☐
10 This person is hard-working.	☐	☐	☐

10 What makes a good and bad friend? Write using words from Activity 9.

A good friend _____.

A bad friend _____.

11  **Listen and match. Then write.**

1  Dan

2  Emma

3  Maddy

4  Robbie

(talkative / not bossy)

(sporty / talkative)

(friendly / shy)

(helpful / hard-working)

1 What's Dan like? He's _____ and _____.

2 What's _____? She's _____ but a little _____.

3 _____? She's _____ but she isn't _____.

4 _____? He's _____ and _____.

12 **Circle.**

1 I like my new teacher (because / but) she's kind.

2 He's hard-working (and / but) clever.

3 My best friend is talkative (and / but) very friendly. She's great!

4 She doesn't get good grades (because / but) she's lazy.

5 He's helpful at home (but / and) he's hard-working in class.

6 She's clever (because / but) very shy. I like her.

13 **Write about two friends at school.**

1 _____

2 _____

14 **Listen and match.**

1 Megan   **2** Seb's mom and dad   **3** The food   **4** Carlos

short   nice   funny   happy   kind   bossy

15 **Imagine you are staying with this family in the United States. Write to a friend.**

From _____

To _____

Subject   My stay in the United States

Dear _____,

I'm having a _____ time here in the United States.

Emily is _____.

She has _____.

Steven is _____.

He has _____.

Their mom is _____.

She has _____.

Love,

_____

Emily   Steven

16  **Write.**

Warm colors = yellow, _____, _____, _____, _____

Cool colors = green, _____, _____, _____, _____

17 **Think and write.**

~~grass~~   ~~a banana~~   a tomato   a hippo   a lake
a lion   a giraffe   an elephant   a peach   the sea

warm colors	**cool colors**
_____a banana_____	_____grass_____
_____	_____
_____	_____
_____	_____
_____	_____

18  **Write.**

short   1500   young   picture
mustache   curly   28   thin

This ¹_____ is of artist Durer from

Germany. Durer painted this picture in

²_____. In this picture he has a long,

³_____ face. He has long, ⁴_____

hair. He has a ⁵_____ beard and a

⁶_____, too. He is a ⁷_____ man.

In this picture he is ⁸_____ years old.

19  **Write.**

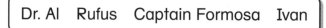

Dr. Al   Rufus   Captain Formosa   Ivan

1    **2**    **3**    **4**

_____   _____   _____   _____

20  **Check (✓).**

1 Who has an emergency?   **2** Why? What is not in the submarine?

a   b   c   a   b   c

☐   ☐   ☐   ☐   ☐   ☐

21 **Find the words in the story and write.**

1 These two words mean "Let's go."   _____

2 Paper with a picture of a town or country on it.   _____

3 These black and white birds can swim.   _____

4 Captain Formosa has only one of these.   _____

5 This looks like a plane with no wings.   _____

6 Moving your body quickly to music.   _____

22 **Imagine. What happens next in the story?**

I think _____.

23 **Be a good friend. What do you say? Number.**

1 Do you want to review for the test?

2 10/10. Good job!

3 Can I help you?

4 I like your drawing.

a

b

c

d

24 **Are you a good friend? Draw or stick a picture of yourself. Then write your own online profile.**

25 **Match.**

1 bald
2 handsome
3 dark hair
4 beautiful
5 a mustache
6 hard-working
7 kind
8 sporty
9 talkative
10 shy

a likes speaking a lot
b quiet and not bossy
c hair under a man's nose
d opposite of lazy
e good at games like soccer and volleyball
f opposite of light hair
g a helpful and friendly person
h "good-looking" (for women)
i no hair
j "good-looking" (for men)

26 **Write.**

straight hair	long hair
beautiful	spiky hair
blue eyes	good-looking
bald	tall

am / is / are	have / has

27 **Write. Then number.**

1 What _____ she look like? _____ tall and has spiky, black hair.

2 What _____ he look like? _____ short and bald.

3 What _____ they look like? _____ beautiful and have long, straight hair.

28 **Unscramble and write questions. Then look at Activity 27 and write the answers.**

a is / like / she / what _____

b they / like / are / what _____

c your / like / what / uncle / is _____

29 **09** **Listen and write.**

> bossy   tall   likes   kind   clever   sporty   name   straight   talkative

SEARCH

My friend

What does she look like?

My friend's ¹_____ is Miki. She's ²_____ and she has

dark, ³_____ hair. She has brown eyes and she wears glasses. She

⁴_____ skirts and colorful T-shirts.

What's she like?

She's ⁵_____ and ⁶_____. She's a bit ⁷_____

but it's OK. I like her because she's funny, ⁸_____, and

⁹_____.

30 **Describe a friend or family member.**

What does he/she look like?

_____

_____

_____

What's he/she like?

_____

_____

_____

_____

2 My life

1 ✎ **Number.**

1 the garbage   **2** my teeth   **3** notes in class   **4** my face

5 my friends   **6** my bed   **7** on time   **8** my room

9 before a test   **10** my homework

a wash   `4`   **b** brush   ☐   **c** make   ☐   **d** clean   ☐

e take   ☐   **f** meet   ☐   **g** do   ☐   **h** be   ☐

i take out   ☐   **j** study   ☐

2 🔟 **Write. Then listen and write ✓ or ✗ for Dan.**

#			Dan	You
1		I <u>brush my teeth</u> in the morning.		
2		I _____ every day.		
3		I _____ before school.		
4		I'm _____ for school every day.		
5		I _____ in class.		
6		I _____ before a test.		
7		I _____ after school.		
8		I _____ every day.		

3 **Look at Activity 2 and write ✓ or ✗ for yourself.**

4 (11) **What should they do before bed? Listen and match. Then write.**

1 Robbie and Emma
2 Emma
3 Robbie
4 Dad
5 Mom

a brush his teeth
b walk the dog
c say good night to their parents
d clean the kitchen
e wash her hair

1 _____

2 _____

3 _____

4 _____

5 _____

5 **What should your family do before bed? Write.**

1 I should _____.

2 My _____ should _____.

3 _____

4 _____

6 (12) **What must they do on Saturday? Listen and match. Then write.**

1 Robbie and Emma
2 Mom and Dad
3 Maddy
4 Dan

a do his homework
b clean their rooms
c take out the garbage
d practice the piano

1 _____

2 _____

3 _____

4 _____

7 Write.

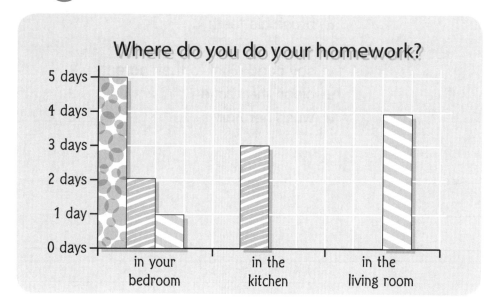

Where do you do your homework?

Matt
Sasha
Jamie
You

1 Matt _____never_____ does his homework in the kitchen.

2 Matt _____ does his homework in his bedroom.

3 Sasha _____ does her homework in her bedroom.

4 Jamie _____ does his homework in the living room.

8 Look at Activity 7 and complete the chart for yourself. Then write.

1 _____ in my bedroom.

2 _____ in the kitchen.

3 _____ in the living room.

9 Find and write.

the dog

Matt

Jamie

Sasha

1 This is _____Jamie's_____ skateboard.   **2** This is _____ ball.

3 This is _____ brother.   **4** This is _____ bike.

10 **Listen and check (✓). Then write.**

What does Mira do each day?

MY WEEK					
	Monday	Tuesday	Wednesday	Thursday	Friday
brush my teeth	✓				
make my bed					
do my homework					
set the table					
take out the garbage					

1 She always brushes her teeth.

2 _____

3 _____ after dinner.

4 _____

5 _____

11 **Listen and write.**

I ¹_____ get up at ²_____.

I ³_____ leave home at ⁴_____.

I ⁵_____ to school or sometimes run!

I ⁶_____ be on ⁷_____.

School starts at ⁸_____, but I

⁹_____ be there at ¹⁰_____.

Today after school, I ¹¹_____ a birthday present

for my mom. It's her birthday tomorrow.

At home, I ¹²_____ set the table. Today is Tuesday,

so I must take out the garbage ¹³_____ bed.

12 Write.

1 He _____goes_____ (go) to school.

   He ____must go____ (go + must) to school.

2 She _____ (watch) TV.

   She _____ (watch + should + not) TV all day.

3 He _____ (make) his bed.

   He _____ (make + should) his bed.

4 She _____ (wash) her face.

   She _____ (wash + should) her face before school.

5 He _____ (do) his homework.

   He _____ (do + must) his homework.

6 She _____ (brush) her hair.

   She _____ (brush + should) her hair.

13 Write.

always	his	must get up	often eat	always eats
should	sometimes sings		usually get up	

I don't like mornings. My big brother ¹_____

gets up at five o'clock. He ²_____ early every day

because he's a farmer. He ³_____ songs in the

morning. ⁴_____ songs are horrible. I can't sleep

after that. I ⁵_____ at six o'clock because I'm

hungry. I like eggs for breakfast but I ⁶_____

toast. Why? Because my brother ⁷_____ all of our

eggs at half past five. He ⁸_____ give me some

but he doesn't. Grrr!

14 **Read and choose ✓ or ✗. Then find and write the hidden word.**

SOCIAL SCIENCE

Health quiz

		✓	✗
1	Milk is good for your teeth and bones.	B	M
2	Healthy people never walk and always use their cars.	E	O
3	An apple – only an apple – is a good, healthy breakfast.	A	N
4	Eating a lot of cake isn't very good for you.	E	T
5	Riding a bike isn't healthy.	Y	S

What's my name?

B_ _ _ _ _ _ !

15 **16** **Read. Then listen and correct six differences. Then circle.**

Application form

We are looking for healthy soccer players for our soccer team.
Write about your day.

ten
I get up at ~~seven~~ o'clock. I have eggs on toast for breakfast. I always

brush my teeth after breakfast. I often play soccer in the afternoon.

After that, I have a shower, eat dinner, and I go to bed at nine o'clock.

Do you think he is a healthy person?   Yes / No

16  **Write.**

1 Captain Formosa always gets up at _____.

2 Then he has his _____.

3 He gives some _____ to the penguins.

4 He usually _____ his map.

5 It's a _____ map of Ice Island.

6 The thieves are _____.

17 **Write.**

| meets his friends   goes swimming   ~~has lunch~~ |
| goes to bed   cleans his room   has dinner |

He has lunch at
half past twelve.

_____

_____

_____

_____

18 **Imagine. What happens next in the story?**

I think _____.

19 ✏️ **Number. Then write.**

What should Sarah give each friend?

a Lucy — Today is my birthday! — **4**

1 a ticket for a show

b John — I'm bored!

2 a text message

c Fiona — I'm sick!

3 some flowers

d Tom — I'm shy!

4 a birthday card

a <u>She should give Lucy a birthday card.</u>

b _____

c _____

d _____

20 ✏️ **Think of four people you know (family or friends). What are they like? What should you give them?**

1 I should give _____.

2 _____

3 _____

4 _____

21 **Match.**

1	be on time	**a**	make something not messy
2	homework	**b**	use water and a toothbrush
3	garbage	**c**	listen and write
4	take notes	**d**	schoolwork to do after school finishes
5	clean	**e**	use water and soap
6	brush my teeth	**f**	opposite of always
7	wash my face	**g**	not early and not late
8	never	**h**	things you don't want
9	study before a test	**i**	maybe four times a week
10	often	**j**	you must do this a lot to get 100%

22 **Unscramble and write. Then number.**

1 day / every / must / you / make / your / bed

_____

2 after / brush / breakfast / teeth / should / they / their

_____

3 help / the / parents / should / we / our / clean / house

_____

4 this / 10 p.m. / homework / must / I / finish / before

_____

a  **b**  **c**  **d**

23 **Look at Activity 22 and number to match the answers.**

a We sometimes help our mom and dad in the house. ☐

b Because I should go to bed at ten. ☐

c I always make my bed. I never forget. ☐

d They usually brush their teeth then and they always brush them before bed. ☐

24 **17** **Listen and write.**

| sometimes | dinner | must | often | always | wash | should | help |

My evenings

In the evening, I ¹_____ do my homework. I ²_____ do

my homework before ³_____. After dinner, I ⁴_____ my

mom clean the table and ⁵_____ the dishes. I ⁶_____

watch TV from 7:30 because my favorite program is on from 7:30 to 8:00.

I ⁷_____ email friends or play on my computer.

I ⁸_____ go to bed at 10:00 but sometimes I'm late.

25 **What do you do in the evenings? Use *should* and *must* to write sentences.**

3 Free time

1 **Match.**

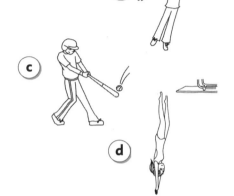

a
b
c
d

1 going shopping

2 throwing

3 hitting

4 catching

5 diving

6 kicking

7 telling jokes

8 trampolining

9 reading poetry

e
f
g
h
i

2 **Write.**

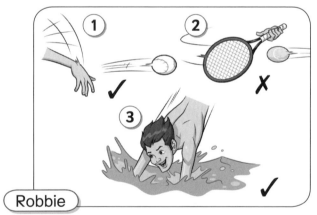

Robbie

Dan

1 I'm good at _____throwing_____.

2 I'm not good at _____.

3 I'm _____.

4 I'm _____

5 I'm _____.

6 I'm _____.

3 18 **Look at Activity 2. Listen and circle who is talking.**

Robbie / Dan

4 Write.

are they're I'm at isn't am good what you

1
¹_____ are you good at?

²_____ good ³_____ throwing.

2
He ⁴_____ good at catching.

Are ⁵_____ good at running?

3
⁶_____ you

⁷_____ at climbing?

4
Yes, I ⁸_____,
but ⁹_____ good
at jumping!

5 Write questions. Then circle for yourself.

1 <u>Are you good at kicking?</u> Yes, I am. / No, I'm not.

2 _____ Yes, I am. / No, I'm not.

3 _____ Yes, I am. / No, I'm not.

4 _____ Yes, I am. / No, I'm not.

6 Write about your friends.

1 (likes) _____

2 (loves) _____

7 Complete the crossword. Then find and write.

I love S _ _ _ _ _ _ _ _ karaoke!

1   2   3   4   5   6

7

¹i	n	-	l	i	n	e		s	k	a	t	i	n	g			
		²			n												
³																	
⁴																	
⁵																	
⁶		c															
⁷		g															

8 Write.   🏆 = is/are good at   ♡ = loves/love   😣 = doesn't/don't like

1 _____

2 _____

3 _____

4 _____

5 _____

6 _____

19 **Sing.** (See Student Book page 38.)

9  **Write.**

YESTERDAY	Robbie	Emma	Maddy and Dan
7:00	sleeping	eating breakfast	walking to school
11:00	studying music	writing a story	swimming
12:00	eating lunch	eating lunch	playing with friends
2:45	having computer class	drawing in class	reading in English class
5:00	playing soccer at school	working on a project	eating ice cream with friends
8:00	singing in the bath	meeting friends	watching TV

1 What was Robbie doing yesterday at 7:00? He was _____.

2 What _____ Maddy and Dan doing yesterday at 11:00?

They were _____.

3 What _____ Emma doing yesterday at 12:00?

She _____ lunch.

4 What _____ Maddy and Dan doing yesterday at 2:45?

They _____ in English class.

5 What _____ Robbie _____ yesterday at _____?

_____ soccer at school.

6 What _____ Emma _____ yesterday at 8:00?

_____.

10  **Write. Then look at Activity 9 and circle.**

1 Was Emma eating breakfast at 7:00? (Yes, she _____. / No, she wasn't.)

2 _____ Maddy and Dan _____ lunch at 12:00?

(Yes, they _____. / No, they _____.)

3 _____ Robbie _____ on a project at 2:45?

(Yes, he was. / No, _____.)

4 _____ Maddy and Dan _____ TV at 8:00?

(Yes, _____. / No, _____.)

11 (20) Read. Then listen and correct six differences.

Dear Grandma,

Action Camp is great! I'm here with Ellie because we both love sports. We go swimming every morning. I love ~~sleeping~~ swimming. I can swim fifty meters underwater now. We have dancing lessons, too. I'm not very good at diving because I feel scared but Ellie can dive from the big diving board. She's fantastic! Ellie and I like trampolining after breakfast and we love playing soccer together in the morning. Ellie is very good at running and hitting the ball.

Mark

12 Look at Activity 11 and write.

1 What does Mark love doing in the morning?

____

2 Can Mark swim? ______________________

3 Is Mark good at diving? ______________________

4 Is Ellie good at diving? ______________________

5 What do Ellie and Mark like doing after lunch?

____

6 Do they like playing tennis? ______________________

13 Write the *–ing* form.

+ *ing*		+ last letter + *ing*		- e + *ing*	
kick	kicking	swim	swimming	dance	dancing
sing	______	hit	______	dive	______
play	______	run	______	ride	______

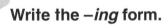

14 Write.

write   writing   play   playing   good at   my

Hi. ¹_____ name's David. I have guitar lessons every

○ week. I love ²_____ the guitar—my teacher is great.

My friend, Melissa, is ³_____ singing and her brother

can ⁴_____ the drums. Last Sunday we were playing

○ songs all day. It was fun! I like ⁵_____ music, too. One day, I

want to ⁶_____ music for movies.

15 Listen to the music and check (✓) for yourself.

1 cool ☐	OK ☐	bad ☐
3 cool ☐	OK ☐	bad ☐
5 cool ☐	OK ☐	bad ☐
7 cool ☐	OK ☐	bad ☐

2 cool ☐	OK ☐	bad ☐
4 cool ☐	OK ☐	bad ☐
6 cool ☐	OK ☐	bad ☐
8 cool ☐	OK ☐	bad ☐

16 Listen again and choose your favorite. Then find that number and read about yourself.

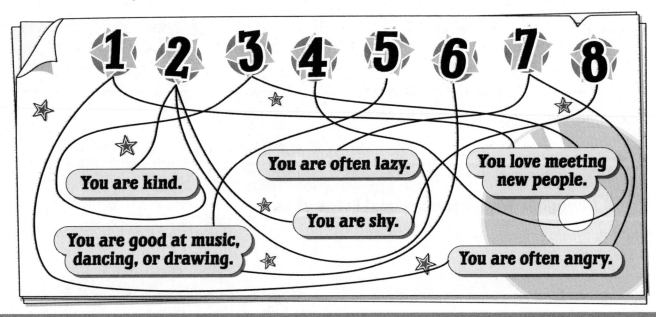

1 2 3 4 5 6 7 8

You are often lazy.

You love meeting new people.

You are kind.

You are shy.

You are good at music, dancing, or drawing.

You are often angry.

17 **Circle T = True or F = False.**

1 Finn is with Dylan and Jenny.   T / F

2 Finn and Dylan have radios.   T / F

3 Ivan and Rufus are reading the map.   T / F

4 Finn isn't watching polar bears.   T / F

5 Finn is good at stopping.   T / F

18 **Read and write.**

Are they good at _____?

Yes, they are.

Is he good at diving?

_____

Does he love _____ the bike?

_____

No, they aren't.

19 **Imagine. What happens next in the story?**

I think _____.

20   **Write your advice.**

take art lessons   join a sports team   join a drama club
start a band   ~~learn computer programming~~

1  I like computers but I'm not good at playing video games.

He should learn computer programming.

2  I love acting and dancing.

_____

3  We like drawing. We love making things.

_____

4  I'm very good at P.E. I love doing headstands!

_____

5  I'm good at playing the guitar. I love singing.

_____

21 **Think of two friends or family members. Suggest hobbies and explain why.**

1 My brother should start a band because he's good at singing and playing the drums.

2 _____

   _____

3 _____

   _____

22 Match.

1 poetry   a an old, popular game for two players
2 a joke   b jumping sport
3 video game   c on a stage, this is a group musical performance
4 diving   d short writing, the words sometimes sound the same
5 shopping   e reading and singing with music from a CD
6 chess   f buying things
7 trampolining   g you can play this on a TV
8 karaoke   h jump arms first into a swimming pool
9 acting   i this should be funny
10 singing in a choir   j speaking and doing actions on a stage

23 **22** **Write. Then listen and circle T = True or F = False.**

1 Sam ♡ 🎸

_____ T / F

2 Anna ✗ ♟

_____ T / F

3 The children 🏆 🎤

_____ T / F

4 Rick 😠 🛹

_____ T / F

5 Bill 😠 🎨

_____ T / F

🏆 = is/are good at
♡ = loves/love
✗ = can't
😠 = doesn't/don't like

24 **Write the missing word. Then write the answer.**

1 What _____ she doing yesterday?

_____

2 What _____ they doing yesterday?

_____

25 **23** **Listen and write.**

My activities

I like ¹_____ tennis. I play tennis at a club. Yesterday, I ²_____

playing in the afternoon. We usually play games on Sunday and we ³_____

on Wednesday. I love swimming, too. I ⁴_____ swimming on Monday and

Thursday. I ⁵_____ swimming in the sea ⁶_____ the summer, too.

At school, I'm ⁷_____ at sports and English. I'm ⁸_____ good at

art ⁹_____ the teacher helps me a lot.

26 **Write about things you like, don't like, and things you can do.**

_____

_____

_____

_____

_____

_____

_____

_____

_____

_____

_____

_____

_____

_____

Around the world

1 (24) **Listen and number.**

a Spain ☐

b The United Kingdom ☐

c Argentina ☐

d Italy ☐

e The United States ☐

f Brazil ☐

g Mexico ☐

h Egypt ☐

i Japan ☐

j Australia ☐

k Korea ☐

l Colombia ☐

m India ☐

n China ☐

2 ✏️ **Complete the crossword. Use the words from Activity 1.**

4 (across) T H E U N I T E D S T A T E S

3 Write.

1 _____ an

old man under _____.

2 _____ two

birds _____ umbrella.

3 _____ an umbrella on _____.

4 _____ cats on _____.

5 _____ monkeys in the sea.

4 Read and write *a*, *some*, or *any*.

1 There are _____ long rivers in the United States.

2 There isn't _____ rain forest in Italy.

3 There aren't _____ giraffes in the United Kingdom.

4 There are _____ old houses in Spain.

5 There's _____ big waterfall in Brazil and Argentina.

5 Read and write.

1 hippos / China / ✗   There aren't any hippos in China.

2 a rain forest / Australia / ✓ _____

3 a snowy mountain / Egypt / ✗ _____

4 elephants / Mexico / ✗ _____

5 beautiful beaches / Spain / ✓ _____

_____

6 Write three things about your country.

1 _____

2 _____

3 _____

7 Find and circle nine words. Then find and write the answer using the letters that aren't circled.

Apyramiducastlesvolcanotcityrstatueacaveltownifarmafactory

Where are they going?

A_____

8 Look and write. Use words from Activity 7.

		The United Kingdom	Spain
1	a _____	✓	✓
2	_____es	✗	✓
3	a _____	✓	✓
4	_____s	✓	✓
5	_____s	✗	✗
6	_____s	✓	✓
7	a _____	✓	✓
8	_____ies	✓	✓
9	a _____	✓	✓

25 **Sing.** (See Student Book page 50.)

9 Look at Activity 8 and write.

1 _____ pyramids _____ Spain?

No, there aren't.

2 _____ castle _____ Spain?

_____

3 _____ volcanoes _____ United Kingdom?

_____

4 _____ caves _____ United Kingdom?

_____

10 **26** Read, guess, and write. Then listen and check your answers.

1 Are there any beaches in Australia?   Yes, there are. _____

2 Is there a rain forest in Korea?   _____

3 Are there any volcanoes in Italy?   _____

4 Are there any volcanoes in Mexico?   _____

5 Is there a mountain taller than 5,000 meters in Japan?   _____

6 Is there a river longer than the Amazon in China?   _____

11 Make your own quiz.

1 Are there any pyramids in Argentina? _____

No, there aren't. _____

2 _____

_____

3 _____

_____

4 _____

_____

12 **Listen and circle.**

1 Mia is in (Brazil / Mexico).

2 Mia is talking to her (grandma / grandpa).

3 Mia is in a (rain forest / city).

4 There are some (beaches / pyramids) in Rio de Janeiro.

5 There's a big (volcano / statue), too.

6 A lot of people in Brazil are good at (dancing / singing).

13 **Write.**

rain forest   river   trees   animals   beautiful   Grandpa

Dear ¹_____,

Hello from the Amazon ²_____ in Brazil!

There are a lot of tall green ³_____ in the

rain forest and some scary ⁴_____,

too! I'm fishing in a ⁵_____ today. I can

see some monkeys! It's very ⁶_____ here.

See you soon!

Mia

14 **Imagine you are on vacation. Write to a friend.**

Hi _____,

I'm in _____.

There are some _____

_____.

There aren't any _____

_____.

_____

15 **28** **Listen and write.**

Come to Greenland!

1 _____ on snowmobiles!

Climb snowy 2 _____!

See 3 _____ and waterfalls of ice! There aren't 4 _____ big cities

here but there are 5 _____ beautiful polar 6 _____ and reindeer in

this cold place. Every 7 _____ in Greenland is an adventure!

Greenland – a world of ice!

16 **Check (✓).**

Is a vacation in Greenland right for you?

1 I like doing sports:
- **A** on snow, ice, and water. ☐
- **B** on grass. ☐

2 I like eating:
- **A** meat and fish. ☐
- **B** fruit. ☐

3 My favorite clothes are:
- **A** a warm coat and a hat. ☐
- **B** shorts and a T-shirt. ☐

4 In my bedroom, there are some pictures of:
- **A** animals. ☐
- **B** famous people. ☐

5 My favorite time of year is:
- **A** winter. ☐
- **B** summer. ☐

a lot of **A**s: Go to Greenland. It's a great place for you.
a lot of **B**s: Don't go to Greenland. Choose a warm place for your vacation.

17   **Read and correct.**

1 Captain Formosa has the map.

_____

2 The captain has a good memory.

_____

3 There are some pyramids on Ice Island.

_____

4 The treasure is under a volcano.

_____

5 There's a cave in Snow Lake.

_____

18 **29** **Listen and circle the correct penguin. Then write.**

1 The penguin is _____

_____.

2 _____

_____

3 _____

_____

19 **Imagine. What happens next in the story?**

I think _____.

20 Choose two teams for an English project. The people should be good at different things.

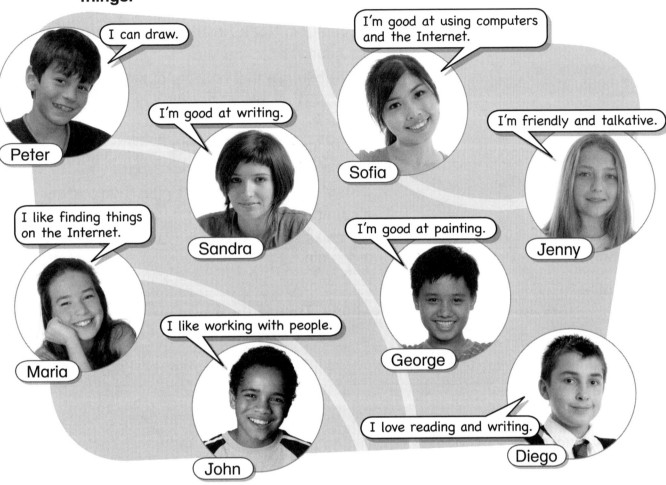

I can draw.

Peter

I'm good at writing.

Sandra

I'm good at using computers and the Internet.

Sofia

I'm friendly and talkative.

Jenny

I like finding things on the Internet.

Maria

I'm good at painting.

George

I like working with people.

John

I love reading and writing.

Diego

Skill	Writing	Art	Computers	Talking
Team A				
Team B				

21 What can you give to a team? Write.

I'm good at _____.

I like _____.

I'm not good at _____.

I don't like _____.

22 ✎ **Match.**

1 a volcano
2 rain forest
3 beach
4 pyramids
5 city
6 Argentina
7 Korea
8 the United States
9 factory
10 farm

a there are some famous ones in Egypt–people made them a long time ago
b a country in North America
c the sand next to the sea
d this is a jungle that has lots of wet weather
e there are animals, fruit, and vegetables in this place
f a country in South America
g people work here and make things
h a lot of people live here—bigger than a town
i a country in Asia
j hot rocks sometimes come out of this type of mountain

23 ✎ **Unscramble and write questions. Then write the answers.**

1 there / is / desert / in / Asia / a

_____

(✔) _____

2 is / rain forest / there / a / Italy / in

_____

(✘) _____

3 are / statues / in / Brazil / there / any

_____

(✔) _____

4 volcanoes / are / there / in / any / Egypt

_____

(✘) _____

5 Japan / castles / in / are / any / there

_____

(✔) _____

(24) **(30)** **Listen and write.**

The river

There's a river near my house. I go there [1]_____ my bike.

[2]_____ aren't [3]_____ people near the river. There

[4]_____ a lot of trees and [5]_____. The birds

[6]_____ in the trees. There are [7]_____ in the river and

[8]_____ they jump. [9]_____ a bridge over the river.

Sometimes, I sit [10]_____ the bridge and read. I love the river.

(25) **Write about a place you know.**

_____

_____

_____

_____

_____

_____

_____

_____

_____

_____

_____

_____

_____

_____

1 Find and circle.

b	r	a	c	e	l	e	t	m	w
i	s	h	y	r	e	x	f	t	h
s	u	n	g	l	a	s	s	e	s
j	m	k	l	q	m	l	a	l	w
j	b	t	o	d	b	l	v	l	i
a	r	f	v	a	z	p	n	a	m
c	e	j	e	w	a	t	c	h	s
k	l	c	s	b	u	n	p	o	u
e	l	g	w	a	l	l	e	t	i
t	a	h	a	n	d	b	a	g	t

2 Write. Use *is* or *are* and words from Activity 1.

1. How much _____ that _____?

2. How much _____ those _____?

3. How much _____ that _____?

4. How much _____ those _____?

3 Listen and circle. What does Maddy buy?

swimsuit / sunglasses

4  **Look and write the prices in words.**

1 _____

  _____

2 _____

  _____

3 _____

  _____

4 _____

  _____

5 _____

  _____

6 _____

  _____

(Prices shown in illustration)
1. $30
2. $21.50
3. $99
4. $112
5. $420
   $55.50

5 32 **The prices in Activity 4 are wrong. Listen and circle the correct price.**

1 **a** $28   **b** $29.90   **c** $29   2 **a** $12.50   **b** $20.50   **c** $15.20

3 **a** $9   **b** $19   **c** $90   4 **a** $212   **b** $200   **c** $121

5 **a** $40.20   **b** $42.20   **c** $42.00   6 **a** $26.50   **b** $25.50   **c** $25.55

6  **Write.**

> course   dollars   how   hundred   much   please

David: Hello. How ¹_____ are those gloves, please?

Shop assistant: They're four ²_____ and fifty cents.

David: And ³_____ much is that watch?

Shop assistant: It's one ⁴_____ dollars.

David: Oh … may I buy the gloves, ⁵_____?

Shop assistant: Yes, of ⁶_____.

7 Number.

a a cheap bracelet ☐

b an old-fashioned watch ☐

c a modern watch ☐

d an expensive bracelet ☐

e baggy jeans ☐

f a tight sweater ☐

① ② $2 ③

④ $199 ⑤ ⑥

8 Write. Use words from Activity 7.

①

These pants are too _____.

② TOYS $5 $40

That _____.

③

This _____.

④

These _____.

9 Write two sentences about your clothes.

long   short   old   baggy   big   small   tight   dark   light   old-fashioned

My green sweater is too tight.

1 _____

2 _____

33 **Sing.** (See Student Book page 62.)

10 **Match the opposites.**

1 expensive
2 modern
3 tight
4 big
5 short

baggy
long
old-fashioned
cheap
small

11 **Write.**

Sky

Lee

1 <u>That jacket is too short.</u>

_____ (short)

2 _____

_____ (baggy)

3 _____

_____ (tight)

4 _____

_____ (long)

12 **Look at Activity 11 and write.**

1 Whose jacket is this? _____. It's hers.

2 Whose pants are these? _____. They're _____.

3 _____ It's Lee's. It's _____.

4 _____ They're Lee's. _____.

13 **Listen and check (✓) the ads the boys talk about.**

¹ BIKE, blue, $123, for a boy 160cm tall.
Tel: 555-9751

² VIDEO GAMES,
20 games for $17.
gamecity@yoohoo.com

³ SCARF, $6.50, red and white.
soccerfan@bkinternet.com

⁴ SKATEBOARD, new, $38.
Tel: 555-3184

⁵ JACKET, $25, white, for a 4-year-old girl.
whiteshop@compuworld.com

14 **Listen again and circle.**

1 The bike in the ad is too (big / expensive / small).

2 The skateboard is too (expensive / big / old-fashioned).

3 Tom wants to buy the (skateboard / video games / bike).

15 **Draw three things. Then write ads for them.**

16  **Write.**

Shorts and a T-shirt   Sailing shoes   A warm jacket   Sunglasses   A swimsuit

Clothes list for sailing lessons

1 _____

Don't wear your favorite clothes. Choose something old and not too expensive.

2 _____

At sea, it's often too windy for summer clothes, even
on sunny days.

3 _____

The sunlight on the water is very bad for your eyes.

4 _____

Our boats are too wet for sneakers and too dangerous for sandals.

5 _____

After the lessons, you can dive from the boat and have fun in the water.

17 (35) **Listen and write.**

		Activity	Clothes
1	Jack	1 _____	warm 2 _____ 3 _____ 4 _____
2	Pete	5 _____ class	6 _____ shoes 7 _____ 8 _____ pants
3	Sally	9 _____ riding	long 10 _____ 11 _____ pants hard 12 _____

18 ✎ **Write.**

1 Where are Jenny, Finn, and Dylan? _____

2 How do Finn and Dylan feel? _____

3 Who is in the fitting room? _____

4 What are they wearing? _____

5 Do the children catch the thieves? _____

6 How do the thieves get away? _____

19 🔘36 **Listen and write the prices. What does Jenny buy?**

Fitting room

Jenny buys the _____.

20 ✎ **Imagine. What happens next in the story?**

I think _____.

21 **What should they wear? Write ✓ or ✗.**

VALUES
Dress correctly for each occasion.

1 I have a wedding this evening.

a light blue dress ☐

blue sneakers ☐

a white belt ☐

a blue cap ☐

white shoes ☐

sunglasses ☐

a dark green hat ☐

a gold bracelet ☐

a swimsuit ☐

2 I have a party tonight.

baggy pants ☐

jeans ☐

a white shirt ☐

a dark green jacket ☐

a red belt ☐

black sneakers ☐

shorts ☐

a black T-shirt ☐

sunglasses ☐

black boots ☐

3 I have a sailing lesson.

tight jeans ☐

a baggy T-shirt ☐

sunglasses ☐

a warm jacket ☐

a yellow scarf ☐

sneakers ☐

baggy jeans ☐

a cap ☐

boots ☐

22 **What do you wear to a wedding or a school party? Write.**

A wedding

1 _____

2 _____

3 _____

4 _____

A school party

1 _____

2 _____

3 _____

4 _____

23 Match.

1	umbrella	a	opposite of modern
2	bracelet	b	you can keep your money and cell phone in here
3	wallet	c	you can wear these on your hands
4	handbag	d	opposite of baggy
5	gloves	e	opposite of expensive
6	short	f	you can use this on rainy days
7	tight	g	opposite of dark
8	light	h	you can keep your money in this
9	cheap	i	opposite of long
10	old-fashioned	j	you can wear one, two, three, or more of these

24 Number to make a dialogue.

a Oh! That's too expensive. I have only twenty dollars. How much are those dark blue jeans?

b Yes, of course. Eight dollars, please.

c Great. May I buy it, please?

d They're eighteen dollars and fifty cents.

e Well, they're cheap, but they're too baggy. I like wearing tight jeans. How much is that scarf?

f The sweater is twenty-one dollars.

g Excuse me. How much is that sweater?

h It's eight dollars.

25 Listen and write. Whose are these?

_____   _____   _____   _____

26 **38** **Listen and write.**

My clothes

My favorite ¹_____ is white with small letters on the ²_____.

It's really cool. My favorite shoes are my ³_____. They're

⁴_____ and black. I don't like my winter boots ⁵_____

they're ⁶_____ and my summer ⁷_____ are

⁸_____ small now. I like my ⁹_____ uniform. I really like

the jacket. It's green and gold. They're my favorite ¹⁰_____.

27 **Write about your clothes.**

_____

_____

_____

_____

_____

_____

_____

_____

_____

_____

_____

_____

_____

6 Party time

1 Write.

		Yesterday, …
1	make	I _____ a sandwich for lunch.
2	have	I _____ dinner at 6:00 p.m.
3	come	I _____ to school by bus.
4	give	I _____ my friend a present.
5	see	I _____ my grandmother.
6	bring	I _____ my lunch to school.
7	meet	I _____ my grandfather.
8	eat	I _____ curry.
9	get	I _____ 100% on a test.
10	sing	I _____ in a choir.

2 Write.

1 Yesterday _____ Dan's birthday. He is twelve now. ☐

2 He _____ a new soccer ball. ☐

3 Robbie _____ Dan some sneakers for a present. ☐

4 The party was fun. Everyone _____ "Happy Birthday." ☐

5 Dan's cousins _____ to the party. ☐

6 There _____ some games in the garden. ☐

7 They _____ pizza and cake after the games. ☐

8 Dan's mom _____ the birthday cake. ☐

3 🔊39 Listen and check (✓) the true sentences in Activity 2.

4  **Write.**

Robbie ¹_____ (have) a birthday party in February. A lot of friends ²_____ (come) to the party. They ³_____ (bring) food, drinks, and presents. Dan ⁴_____ (give) Robbie a wallet for his birthday. Emma didn't bring a present because she ⁵_____ (make) a very big cake for Robbie.

Robbie's party

5  **Write.**

Emma had a birthday party in July. Maddy came, but Kipper didn't ¹_____. Robbie brought a small cake from a store. He's not good at cooking so he didn't ²_____ it. They didn't ³_____ songs but there was music so everyone danced. There were sandwiches but they didn't ⁴_____ a lot of drinks.

Emma's party

6  **Look at the two pictures above and check (✓) Robbie or Emma.**

	Robbie	Emma
1 It was sunny.	☐	☐
2 Friends sang but didn't play music.	☐	☐
3 There was a big cake.	☐	☐
4 Maddy didn't come to the party.	☐	☐
5 Seven children came to the party.	☐	☐
6 They had a lot of drinks.	☐	☐

7 (40) **Listen and match.**

December

		1	2 [b]	3	4	5
6	7	8	9	10	11 [ ]	12
13 [ ]	14	15	16	17 [ ]	18	19
20 [ ]	21	22	23	24	25 [ ]	26
27	28	29	30	31		

a Christmas

b Taylor's BIRTHDAY

c Mom's Birthday

d Party at School

e Soccer Club Party

f Dance Show

8 **Write the date from Activity 7.**

1 Annabel went to a party at school on <u>December 20th</u>.

2 She had a big meal with her family for Christmas on _____.

3 She said "Happy Birthday!" to her mom on _____.

4 She said "Happy Birthday!" to her cousin on _____.

5 She went to her soccer club party on _____.

6 She went to a dance show on _____.

9 **Write about something you did last month. What did you do and when did you do it?**

> I went to the zoo on April 12th.

_____

_____

(41) **Sing.** (See Student Book page 74.)

10 Listen and write the dates.

Place	Date	Activities
China	July _____	go on a boat; see a lot of tall buildings
	July _____	walk on the Great Wall of China
Korea	July _____	meet some new friends; have a party
	July _____	go to an island; play on a beach
Japan	July _____	see a temple; eat a lot of fish
	July _____	go on a fast train; climb Mount Fuji

11 Look at Activity 10 and write.

1 On July _____ they went to _____. They _____ on a boat and _____ a lot of tall buildings.

2 On July _____ they _____ on the Great Wall of China.

3 On July _____ they went to _____. They _____ some new friends and _____ a party.

4 On July _____ they went to an island and _____ on a beach.

5 On July _____ they went to _____. They _____ a temple and _____ a lot of fish.

6 On July _____ they went on a fast train and _____ Mount Fuji.

12 **43** **Listen and number.**

13 **43** **Listen again and complete for Lucy.**

	Lucy	You
Where was the party?	the ¹_____beach_____	
How was the weather?	²_____ but ³_____	
What food was there?	⁴_____, salad, and strawberries	
What games were there?	⁵_____	
Did you dance?	⁶_____, we_____.	
Did you sing?	⁷_____, we _____.	

14 **Imagine you went to a party. Complete the table in Activity 13 for yourself. Then write full sentences below.**

The party was at the beach. The weather was sunny but windy.

_____

_____

15 (44) **Listen and check (✓) the things that were on the *Mayflower*.**

a doctor ☐	horses ☐	a teacher ☐	hats ☐
hens ☐	books ☐	cows ☐	clothes ☐
pigs ☐	beds ☐		

16 **Write.**

My Journal, by Samuel Payne

December 22nd, 1661

Our first months here ¹_____ (be) very bad. My parents ²_____ (be) very thin because there was no food. I ³_____ (be) thin, too. We were very scared.

In the summer, I often ⁴_____ (go) to the river with my Native American friends. I ⁵_____ (be) good at fishing! Then, in the fall, we ⁶_____ (have) a big Thanksgiving party. We ⁷_____ (eat) good food and said thank you to the Native Americans for their help.

17 **Write the end of Samuel's journal in Activity 16. Use the words in the box.**

songs and games fifty settlers meat	
fish from the river vegetables from our farm	

At the party there were ninety Native Americans and _____.

_____

_____

_____

_____

18 Number the sentences in order.

a   Jenny and Finn got in the snowmobile.

b   Jenny said, "We can catch them!"

c   The thieves were in their boat.

d   The thieves went into a cave in the sea.

e   The thieves went into a store.

f   The children went to the entrance of the cave on Snow Mountain.

19 Read and draw.

There was a mountain. It was snowy. There were two penguins in the sea. There was a statue of a man at the top of the mountain. There was a big cave in the mountain. The boat was in the cave. The boat was small and red. Rufus and Ivan were in the boat.

20 Imagine. What happens next in the story?

I think _____.

21  **Match.**

Problems

1 I have a sailing lesson. What should I wear?

2 I don't know the meaning of a word.

3 I'm not good at writing.

4 I don't have money to buy a birthday present.

5 I want to play soccer. I'm not good at it.

6 I have a test and feel nervous.

7 I can't remember vocabulary easily.

8 My clothes are too tight.

Solutions

a Eat healthy food only.

b Write about things you like.

c Make lists of new words.

d Wear old jeans, a T-shirt, and a warm jacket.

e Don't worry. Make a birthday card.

f Use a dictionary.

g Invite a friend to review with you.

h Don't worry. Play for fun.

22 **Think and write other solutions to the problems in Activity 21.**

Problem 1: _____

Problem 2: _____

Problem 3: _____

Problem 4: _____

Problem 5: _____

Problem 6: _____

Problem 7: _____

Problem 8: _____

23 **Write about a problem you had before and how you solved it.**

Problem: _____

Solution: _____

(24) **Write the missing words.**

1	first	→	second	→	third	→	
2	first	→	third	→	fifth	→	
3	tenth	→	fifteenth	→	twentieth	→	
4	third	→	tenth	→	seventeenth	→	
5	first	→		→	twenty-first	→	thirty-first
6	thirteenth	→	tenth	→		→	fourth
7	twenty-fourth	→	twelfth	→		→	third
8		→	fourth	→	eighth	→	sixteenth

(25) **Write about what you did last week.**

1 (come) - <u>Last week I came home from school early every day.</u>

2 (give) - _____

3 (see) - _____

4 (eat) - _____

5 (get) - _____

6 (go) - _____

(26) **Circle.**

Yesterday, I ¹(went / brought) to a birthday party. I ²(made / met) some old friends and ³(make / made) many new friends at the party. The party was in my town's park. We ⁴(had / have) lots of food and drink and ⁵(played / play) lots of games. We didn't ⁶(bring / brought) the food but we ⁷(ate / eat) it! We ⁸(was / were) very tired after the party but it ⁹(was / were) a fantastic day.

(27) **Look at Activity 26 and write.**

1 When was the birthday party? _____

2 Where was the party? _____

28 (45) **Listen and write.**

A fun party

I ¹_____ to a birthday party at my school. The school was 50 years

old. Parents and grandparents ²_____ to the school party. There

³_____ drinks and food. We ⁴_____ a lot. The teachers

⁵_____ and we ⁶_____ games outside. In the evening,

we ⁷_____ and talked with friends. The bakery in our town

⁸_____ a very big cake and ⁹_____ it to the school.

It ¹⁰_____ a fun party!

29 **Write about a fun party you went to.**

_____

_____

_____

_____

_____

_____

_____

_____

_____

_____

_____

School

1 (46) **Listen and write.**

scary boring easy difficult funny romantic interesting exciting

The first lesson at school was ¹_____. The second and third lessons were

²_____. There was an ³_____ game in the fourth lesson.

Lunch was ⁴_____. The lessons after lunch were ⁵_____. In

the last lesson, we read some poems. Some were ⁶_____, some were

⁷_____, and some were ⁸_____.

2 (47) **Listen and write for Maddy. Use words from Activity 1.**

1 Maddy: _____*boring*_____
   You: _____

2 Maddy: _____
   You: _____

3 Maddy: _____
   You: _____

4 Maddy: _____
   You: _____

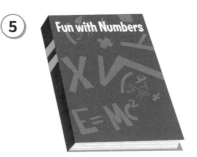

5 Maddy: _____
   You: _____

6 Maddy: _____
   You: _____

3 **Write a word under each book in Activity 2 for yourself.**

4 **Read. Then match.**

My first day at school was scary. I was only five and there were a lot of big children in the school. The lessons were very difficult. My teacher was kind but I was very sad!

1 Was Emma's first day at school scary?
2 Was she four?
3 Were there a lot of big children?
4 Were the lessons easy?
5 Was her teacher kind?
6 Was she sad?

a No, she wasn't.
b Yes, he was.
c Yes, it was.
d No, they weren't.
e Yes, she was.
f Yes, there were.

5 **Unscramble and write questions about your first day at school. Then write the answers.**

1 you / how / were / old
_____
_____

2 your / kind / was / teacher
_____
_____

3 there / scary / any / were / things
_____
_____

4 you / were / happy
_____
_____

6 **Write about the first time you did your favorite sport.**

How old were you?   Who was with you?   Were you happy?
Was it exciting/scary/easy/difficult?

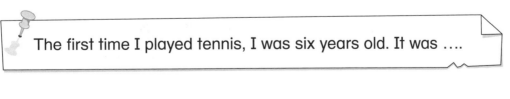

The first time I played tennis, I was six years old. It was ….

_____
_____

7 Find and circle six words. Then unscramble the letters that aren't circled.

IGEOGRAPHYSNMUSICSCIENCELMATHGARTEHHISTORY

What was your favorite subject last year?

8 48 Write. Then listen and circle T = True or F = False.

✓ = was/were   ✗ = wasn't/weren't

1 + ✓ boring   P.E. and geography were boring.   T / F

2 ✗ easy   _____   T / F

3 + ✓ fun   _____   T / F

4 ✗ interesting   _____   T / F

5 + ✗ difficult   _____   T / F

6 ✓ exciting   _____   T / F

9 Write three sentences about your lessons last week.

1 Science was _____.

2 Math _____.

3 _____

7 49 Sing. (See Student Book page 86.)

10 **Listen and circle. Then write.**

Dan's homework diary				
Monday	**Tuesday**	**Wednesday**	**Thursday**	**Friday**
math	history	English	music	music
computer science	geography	science	art	P.E.

1 Did Dan have computer science homework on Monday? _____

2 Did Dan have geography homework on Tuesday? _____

3 Did Dan have English homework on Wednesday? _____

4 Did Dan have art homework on Thursday? _____

5 Did Dan have music homework on Friday? _____

11 **Write.**

Maddy's homework diary				
Monday	**Tuesday**	**Wednesday**	**Thursday**	**Friday**
music	English	computer science	math	geography art
easy	easy	boring	difficult	interesting

1 Maddy's homework on Tuesday was _____.

Was it difficult? _____

2 Was Maddy's homework on Thursday difficult? _____

3 Was Maddy's homework on Wednesday interesting?

_____

4 Maddy's homework on Friday was _____ and _____.

Was it boring? _____

5 Was Maddy's homework on Monday easy? _____

12 **Write.**

Did you have homework yesterday? _____

Was it difficult? _____

13 Read and circle.

Jack: Hi, Suzy. Were you on your school trip yesterday?

Suzy: No, not yesterday. We went on Thursday. We were in London. There were some beautiful statues and some interesting pictures, too.

Jack: Why were you there?

Suzy: It was an art trip. We're learning about artists from around the world, and London has art from lots of different countries: Egypt, China, Spain, France, the United States, and the United Kingdom of course.

Jack: Was it an interesting day?

Suzy: Yes, it was. It was very interesting but we were very tired after the trip. There was a lot of walking!

Jack: Walking?! I always go to London by train.

Suzy: Yes, we went by train and then by bus. But in the afternoon there weren't any buses and it was a very long walk!

1 Suzy's school trip was on (Thursday / yesterday).

2 There were some beautiful (statues / houses).

3 It was an (art / geography) trip.

4 It was a very (interesting / boring) day.

5 The children were (excited / tired) after the trip.

6 There weren't any (buses / trains) in the afternoon.

14 Write about your school trip.

My class went on a school trip (when?) _____. It was a (what

subject?) _____ trip. We went to (where?) _____.

It was very (boring/interesting/exciting/scary) _____ because

_____.

15 Write questions. Then answer for Tara.

1 any other children / on your farm ✗

<u>Were there any other children on your farm?</u> <u>No, there weren't.</u>

2 any horses / on your farm ✓

_____ _____

3 a radio / in your house ✓

_____ _____

4 any teachers / near your house ✗

_____ _____

16 ⟨51⟩ Listen and write.

Star Interview!

And then we went to the United States, and I went to ¹_____ there.

²_____ **you happy at your new school?**

No, I ³_____. It was very ⁴_____ in a class

with lots of other children.

Were your teachers good?

Yes, they were. But the ⁵_____ and English lessons were too

⁶_____, and the ⁷_____ and geography lessons were too

⁸_____.

What was your favorite subject?

⁹_____—I was in the basketball team. It was very ¹⁰_____.

17 Do you want to go to Tara's school? Why / Why not? Write.

_____

_____

 **Write.**

| cave | have | see | geography | isn't | too | thieves |

1 Where's the _____?

2 I can't _____ it! It _____ here.

3 You're good at _____.

4 Look, the _____!

5 We _____ the treasure.

6 We're _____ late.

19 **Check (✓).**

1 Who has the treasure?   **2** What didn't the kids find?

20 **Circle.**

1 I'm (good at / can't see) P.E.

2 A (cave / statue) is a hole in a mountain that people can go into.

3 He's never early and never on time. He's always (exciting / late).

4 A (treasure / statue) looks like a man or woman but is hard and not real.

5 Bungee jumping is (careful / scary).

21  **Imagine. What happens next in the story?**

I think _____.

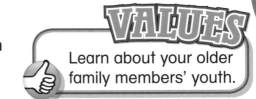

Learn about your older family members' youth.

22 **Unscramble and write questions about an older family members' youth.**

1 was / what / favorite / your / food _____

2 color / what / favorite / your / was _____

3 favorite / who / singer / was / your _____

4 easy / you / was / for / math _____

5 star / was / your / who / movie / favorite _____

6 instrument / you / play / did / an _____

7 movies / like / scary / you / did _____

8 was / what / subject / your / favorite _____

9 you / fun / for / school / was _____

10 P.E. / at / you / good / were _____

23 **Answer the questions in Activity 22 for yourself today.**

1 <u>My favorite food is pizza.</u> _____

2 _____

3 _____

4 _____

5 _____

6 _____

7 _____

8 _____

9 _____

10 _____

24  **Match.**

1 difficult
2 boring
3 funny
4 scary
5 exciting
6 history
7 geography
8 computer science
9 music
10 math

a studying using technology
b studying countries, mountains, and rivers
c studying sound made by instruments
d opposite of interesting
e opposite of easy
f studying with numbers
g jokes should be this
h studying things from long ago
i this is a good, fun feeling
j dark places can be this

25 **Write.**

Were you at home?	Yes, I was.	No, I ¹_____.
²_____ he/she happy?	Yes, he/she was.	No, he/she wasn't.
Was it interesting?	Yes, it ³_____.	No, it wasn't.
Were we tired?	Yes, we were.	No, we ⁴_____.
⁵_____ they funny?	Yes, they were.	No, they weren't.
Was ⁶_____ a cake?	Yes, there was.	No, there wasn't.
Were there any boys?	Yes, there ⁷_____.	No, there weren't.

26 **Write.**

David: My school was a tennis school.

Interviewer: ¹_____ there other lessons, too?

David: Yes, there were—math, science, English, and history. But they ²_____ only in the morning. There ³_____ tennis lessons every afternoon.

Interviewer: ⁴_____ it a good school?

David: Yes, it was. My sister ⁵_____ happy there, too. Her favorite subject was a but there ⁶_____ much time for art classes because we ⁷_____ practicing tennis every day. It ⁸_____ a great school for a tennis player!

27 (52) **Listen and write.**

My favorite subjects last year

My favorite subjects last year were English, P.E., and [1]_____.

[2]_____ was good because we read a lot of [3]_____

poems. Science was [4]_____ but the teacher [5]_____

very good. Her classes were [6]_____. She's my favorite teacher.

[7]_____ was fun [8]_____ I'm good at sports. Wednesday

was my [9]_____ day because we played sports all afternoon. P.E. was

[10]_____ because there were no tests.

28 **Write about your favorite subjects last year.**

_____

_____

_____

_____

_____

_____

_____

_____

_____

_____

_____

_____

_____

1 **Write the nationalities in the crossword.**

1 Korea
2 Egypt
3 Japan
4 the United States
5 Argentina
6 Italy
7 Colombia
8 China
9 India
10 Spain
11 Mexico
12 Brazil
13 the United Kingdom
14 Australia

1 K O R E A N

2 **53** **Listen and match.**

1	Nicole Kidman	Argentina	tennis player
2	J. K. Rowling	Australia	writer
3	Rafael Nadal	the United States	singer
4	Lionel Messi	Spain	soccer player
5	Beyonce	the United Kingdom	movie star

3 **Choose two people from Activity 2. Write about them.**

> Nicole Kidman is an Australian movie star.

1 _____

2 _____

4 **54** **Listen and match.**

International Singing Contest

5 **Look at Activity 4 and write.**

1 Where's she from? She's from _____. She's _____.

2 Is he Brazilian? _____. He's from Brazil. He's _____.

3 Is she Egyptian? _____. She's from _____.

She's _____.

4 Where's he from? He's from _____. He's _____.

5 Is she from Argentina? _____. She's from _____.

She's _____.

6 Where's he from? He's from _____. He's _____.

6   **Find and circle ten jobs. Then write.**

c	o	w	b	o	y	a	c	t	o	r
d	s	a	f	a	j	g	p	t	h	u
e	o	i	k	j	r	k	c	j	i	s
y	l	t	e	s	a	i	l	o	r	p
q	d	e	l	o	a	n	c	e	r	y
u	i	r	s	f	i	g	a	c	t	o
e	e	r	m	b	q	d	n	p	c	o
e	r	s	c	i	e	n	t	i	s	t
n	c	m	u	s	i	c	i	a	n	x

(1) _____

(2)  _____

(3)  _____

(4)  _____

(5)  _____

(6)  _____

(7)  _____

(8)  _____

(9)  _____

(10)  _____

7 **Look and write.**

~~Saturday~~   three thirty   the winter   December   Tuesday
the afternoon   seven o'clock   August 25th   1995   night

in	on	at
	Saturday	

8 〈56〉 **Listen and number.**

9 **Write. Then number.**

1 Yao Ming is _____. He's from China.

He's the man _____ played basketball in the
United States.

A movie _____ was made in 2004 tells
the story of his first year in the NBA.

2 Was she _____?

Yes, she was. She was queen of Egypt.

In 51 BC she was the woman _____ ruled Egypt.

A movie _____ was made in 1999 tells
Cleopatra's life story.

3 Where's he from?

He's from Brazil. He's _____.

He's the soccer player _____ Brazilians call King Pele.

A movie _____ was called "Pele Forever" was
made in 2004.

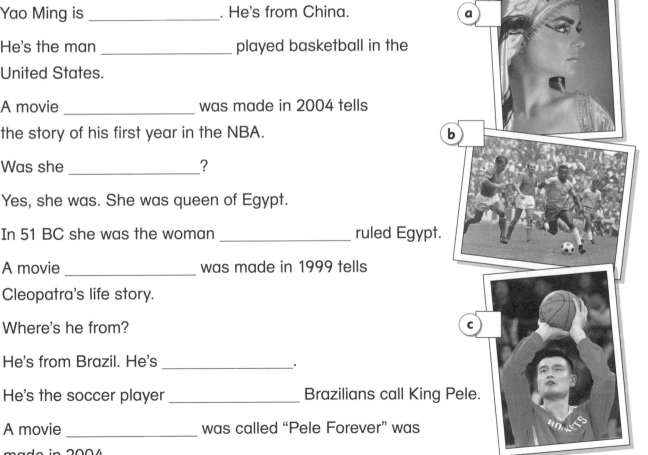

10 (57) **Read. Then listen and number.**

TV Today!

a ☐   **7:30 The Chat Show**
Steve Kilmer talks to young
movie star, Ethan Davis.

b ☐   **8:00 Today in Sport**
All the big games: soccer,
basketball, tennis!

c ☐   **9:00 The Island**
Twelve people are living on a
small island. Life isn't easy!

11   **Write.**

> water   days   famous   king   Chinese   exciting

1 The tennis game is very _____.

2 The players in the game are Spanish and _____.

3 The movie star was a _____ in his first movie.

4 The young actor is very _____ all around the world.

5 On the island, there isn't any clean _____.

6 The girl got the fruit two _____ ago.

12   **Write about your favorite TV show.**

My favorite TV show is _____.

It is _____.

13 Circle.

¹(In / On / At) the winter, it's dark after school. I come home ²(in / on / at)
3:30 and do my homework. Then I play video games. ³(Last / Yesterday / Three)
year, my favorite video game was *Nintendogs* but the game that I like now is
Guitar Hero. *Guitar Hero* is a game that is popular with my friends. Two months
⁴(last / ago / then), I wasn't very good at ⁵(play / player / playing) the game.
Some of the music is very difficult but now I'm a good ⁶(play / player / playing).
I often play ⁷(in / on / at) the evening with my friends and ⁸(in / on / at)
Saturday and Sunday, too.

14 Read the puzzle. Then circle ✔ = True or ✗ = False in the quiz and
write to find the answer.

This is a puzzle about a cowboy who lived in Texas.
Four days ago, the cowboy went to the city on
Friday. Yesterday, he went home on Friday. How?

Technology Quiz...

1	There were video games a hundred years ago.	✔ We	✗ The
2	There were video games in 1940.	✔ can	✗ horse's
3	Mario is a famous video game character.	✔ name	✗ act
4	Before the books and films, Harry Potter was a video game.	✔ in	✗ was
5	In FIFA video games, you play soccer.	✔ Friday	✗ films

1 ___The___   2 _____   3 _____   4 _____   5 _____

15  **Match.**

1 How does Rufus feel in Picture 1?
2 What does the penguin do?
3 How do Rufus and Ivan feel in Picture 3?
4 Who arrives in the submarine?
5 What is the statue?
6 Who says, "Good job, penguins!"

a Jenny
b Captain Formosa
c He feels happy.
d It scares the thieves.
e They feel scared.
f It's a golden penguin.

16  **Draw your favorite character and write about him/her.**

1 My favorite character is _____.

2 (He / She) has _____.

3 (He / She) is _____.

4 (He / She) likes _____.

17  **Imagine. What happens next to the characters?**

I think _____.

18 **Write. Who is the best role model?**

Be a good role model for others.

 **Gwyneth** always works hard at school and usually arrives on time. Her mother works all day so Gwyneth usually helps a lot around the house. She cleans her room and makes breakfast for her younger brother.

Marcela is never on time and always late. She sometimes works hard at school but doesn't like to clean her room or help around the house, so she never does that.

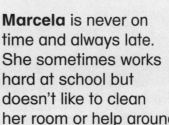

 **Rob** is always on time. He usually works hard at school and does his homework. He always helps at home. He takes out the garbage and cleans his room.

Harry is usually on time but is sometimes late for class. He sometimes works hard at school and sometimes helps at home, but he really likes watching movies.

	arrives on time	works hard at school	helps at home
Gwyneth	u		
Marcela			
Rob			
Harry			

a = always
u = usually
s = sometimes
n = never

The best role model is: _____

19 **Are you a good role model? Write about yourself.**

I _____ arrive on time. _____

_____

20 **What should you do to be better?**

I should help at home.

I should _____.

21  **Match.**

1 a Mexican actor

2 an American cowboy

3 an Italian spy

4 an Indian soldier

5 a Japanese musician

6 an Egyptian king

7 a British waiter

8 a Brazilian sailor

9 a Chinese actor

10 a Korean scientist

a a person from a country in Asia who fights

b a singer or guitar player who is from an island country in Asia

c a rich person who is from a country in north Africa

d a person from a country near the United States who works on a stage

e a man from the United States who works with animals

f a person from a big country in Asia who works on a stage

g a person from a country near Japan who is good at science

h a restaurant worker who is from an island country in Europe

i a person who lives on a ship and comes from a country in South America

j a person from Europe who watches what some people do, then tells other people

22 **Look at Activity 21 and write.**

1 Is the soldier from Brazil?   No, the soldier is from India.

2 Where's the sailor from?   _____

3 Who's from Korea?   _____

4 Is the king from Italy?   _____

5 Are the spy and the waiter from Europe?   _____

6 Where's the musician from?   _____

23 **Write the sentences using *that* or *who*.**

1 a Chinese restaurant / I went to / was very good

_____

2 was good-looking / a Mexican actor / I met

_____

24 **58** **Listen and write.**

My entertainment

My favorite entertainment is ¹_____ TV. I love watching movies at

²_____. I often watch one ³_____ many times. I like

watching movies ⁴_____ are in English. My favorite

⁵_____ is Johnny Depp because he's funny. I ⁶_____

to music, too. I download ⁷_____ from the Internet. I love

⁸_____ music. I like playing many ⁹_____ and play with

my ¹⁰_____ in the park.

25 **Write about your favorite entertainment.**

_____
_____
_____
_____
_____
_____
_____
_____
_____
_____
_____

Goodbye

 1 **Circle T = True or F = False.**

1 The thieves are having a party.   T / F

2 The children helped Captain Formosa stop the thieves.   T / F

3 The children have some food.   T / F

4 The children are now studying the moon with Dr. Al.   T / F

5 Captain Formosa is in his submarine.   T / F

6 Captain Formosa is living on Ice Island with the penguins now.   T / F

 2 **Circle.**

a

1 Whose is this?

It's (Dr. Al's / Captain Formosa's).

2 What did Dylan see with this in Unit 1?

He saw (Captain Formosa / Rufus) on the submarine.

b

3 Who used these?

(Jenny and Finn / The thieves) used them.

4 Where did they buy them?

They bought them in (a store / the Old Harbor Inn).

c

5 Who had this on the mountain?

(Finn / Ivan) had this on the mountain.

6 What did he use it for?

He used it for talking to (Dylan / Rufus).

d

7 Whose is this?

It's (Captain Formosa's / Dylan's).

8 What should be in it?

The (Golden Penguin / treasure map) should be in it.

3  Write.

1 Were there any penguins on Ice Island? _____

2 Was there a statue on Ice Island? _____

3 Were there any pyramids on Ice Island? _____

4 Was there a castle on Ice Island? _____

4  Circle.

1 What's Maddy like? (Unit 1)
   She's (clever but lazy / kind and funny).

2 What was Maddy doing in Unit 2?
   She was (taking out the garbage / doing her homework).

3 What's Robbie good at? (Unit 3)
   He's good at (reading poetry / kicking balls).

4 What was Robbie doing in Unit 2?
   He was (studying before a test / playing computer games).

5 What does Emma look like? (Unit 1)
   She has (straight / spiky) hair and glasses.

6 Emma loves shopping, but what was very expensive? (Unit 5)
   The (scarf / jacket) was very expensive.

7 How much was the thing that was expensive? (Unit 5)
   It was (one hundred and twenty-four dollars / twelve dollars).

8 What was Emma doing in Unit 3?
   She was (telling jokes / reading a book).

9 What does Kipper love doing? (Units 1, 2, and 3)
   He/She loves (eating fish / catching birds).

10 What does Dan look like? (Unit 1)
   He has spiky hair and (brown / green) eyes.

11 What was scary on the bus? (Unit 7)
   A (green / blue) hand was scary on the bus.

12 What was Dan doing in Unit 8?
   He was watching a (basketball / soccer) game.

13 Who's the man who must watch the soccer game because he can't walk? (Unit 8)
   He's (Carlos / Mario).

14 Is Carlos from the United States? (Unit 8)
   No, he isn't. He's (Mexican / Spanish).

5 (59) **Listen and write.**

a	March 1st	
b		Spain
c	March 30th	
d	April 29th	
e		Mexico
f		Argentina
g	June 21st	
h		Korea
i	July 8th	

Japan
China
Italy
the United Kingdom
the United States

6 **Complete your school timetable. What do you think about each subject?**

	Monday	Tuesday	Wednesday	Thursday	Friday
morning					
easy/difficult/ interesting/boring					
afternoon					
easy/difficult/ interesting/boring					

7 **Write about your daily routine.**

I always make my bed in the morning.

1 I always _____.

2 I often _____.

3 I usually _____.

4 I sometimes _____.

5 I never _____.

8 🖊 **Write.**

1 Yesterday, I _____.

2 Yesterday, I didn't _____.

9 🖊 **Draw your favorite place. Then write.**

There's a _____.

There isn't a _____.

There are some _____.

There aren't any _____.

10 🖊 **Draw or stick a picture of your favorite famous person. Then write.**

What does he/she look like?

_____

Why do you like him/her?

_____

What is he/she good at?

_____

Where is he/she from?

_____

This is _____.

(He's / She's) (a / an) _____.

Welcome

Two days ago was Saturday.

I played tennis on Monday morning.

He/She danced at the party on Friday evening.

They went to the movies on Saturday afternoon.

Unit 1 Friends

What does he/she look like?	He's/She's good-looking. He/She has straight, dark hair and brown eyes.
What do they look like?	They're tall and good-looking. They have short, light hair and blue eyes.

He/She doesn't have light hair.
They don't have light hair.

What's he/she like?	He's/She's sporty and he's/she's clever.
	He's/She's bossy but hard-working.

I like him/her because he's/she's kind.

Unit 2 My life

You must brush your teeth. *(Order)*

You should brush your teeth. *(Advice)*

I never brush my teeth.

He sometimes brushes his teeth.

She usually brushes her teeth.

They often brush their teeth.

We always brush our teeth.

Unit 3 Free time

What's he/she good at?	He's/She's good at hitting.
What are they good at?	They're good at hitting.
He/She isn't good at catching. / They aren't good at catching.	
What does he/she like/love doing?	He/She likes/loves going shopping.

What were you doing yesterday at 7:00?	I was going to school.
What was he/she doing yesterday at 7:00?	He/She was going to school.
What were they doing yesterday at 7:00?	They were going to school.
Were you going to school?	Yes, I was. / No, I wasn't.
Was he/she going to school?	Yes, he/she was. / No, he/she wasn't.
Were they going to school?	Yes, they were. / No, they weren't.

Unit 4 Around the world

There's a rain forest in Brazil.

There isn't a rain forest in Korea.

There are some penguins in Argentina.

There aren't any penguins in Italy.

Is there a pyramid in the city?	Yes, there is. / No, there isn't.
Are there any beaches in Australia?	Yes, there are some beautiful beaches in Australia.
Are there any volcanoes in the United Kingdom?	No, there aren't.

Unit 5 Shopping

How much is this/that jacket?	It's ninety dollars and fifty cents.
How much are these/those sunglasses?	They're thirty dollars.

Whose watch is this?		Whose pens are these?	
It's	Maddy's. mine. yours. his. hers.	They're	Dan's. mine. yours. his. hers.

Unit 6 Party time

I made a cake.	
I didn't make a cake.	

Where did you go?	I went to Ghana.
When did you go to Ghana?	I went on August 1st.
What did you see?	I saw giant butterflies.

Unit 7 School

Was it interesting?	Yes, it was. / No, it wasn't.
Was there an alien in it?	Yes, there was. / No, there wasn't.
Were there any exciting stories?	Yes, there were. / No, there weren't.

Did you have computer science on Tuesday?	Yes, I did. / No, I didn't.
Was math difficult?	Yes, it was. / No, it wasn't. It was easy.

Unit 8 Entertainment

Is he/she from the United States?	Yes, he/she is.	No, he/she isn't.
Where's he/she from?	He's/She's from Argentina.	He's/She's Argentinian.
Where are they from?	They're from Australia.	They're Australian.

He's a cowboy.	He likes playing the guitar.	He's a cowboy who likes playing the guitar.
It's an American movie.	It's very famous.	It's an American movie that's very famous.